THE ROLE OF PRIVATE EQUITY IN COMPANIES' GROWTH A Practical Case: Chili S.p.A.

Mauro Tommaso De Candia

I0492582

1

INDEX

INTRODUCTION

The world financial and economic crises, that started in 2008 and it is still ongoing, leads the economic scenario in which Italian SMEs[1] operate. SMEs play a significant role in the Italian economy, being a generator of employment and income and, as a consequence, of growth. At the present time, they have been hit by the global crises in many ways; for instance, in addition to the reduction of sales, companies have a very limited access to credit, payment delays on receivables has increased and suppliers ask for instant payments.

Due to SMEs' importance for the recovery of the Italian economy, it seemed to me important to examine, in the dissertation that follows, a way that gives them the possibility to grow: private equity. Private equity, and in particular expansion capital transactions, can be a possible way to get out of the crises, through the creation of value.

Therefore, in the first chapter, I will present several approaches that private equity funds use to create value in portfolio companies. Afterwards, in the second chapter, I will examine the case of an expansion capital operation, recently performed by Antares Private Equity[2], an Italian private equity firm: Chili S.p.A.[3]

CHAPTER 1. THE MAIN FEATURES OF PRIVATE EQUITY INVESTMENTS

1.1 Definition of private equity

Private equity investments are temporary acquisitions, performed by a financial investor, of a stake in the equity capital of private companies[4] aimed at creating a capital gain in the medium-long term.

When promoting members decide to create a private equity fund, their objective is to gain a return by increasing the value of companies in which they invest. The promoting members of the private equity firm can raise funds both from institutional investors such as pension funds, banks, insurance companies and family offices and from individuals.

Once the funds has been raised, the management team starts the investment process that leads to the performance of investments in target companies. Moreover, the management team of the fund monitors and supports portfolio companies. Finally, once the objective of creating value within the portfolio companies has been achieved, the fund will proceed to the divestment of the stakes, seeking to maximize capital gains.

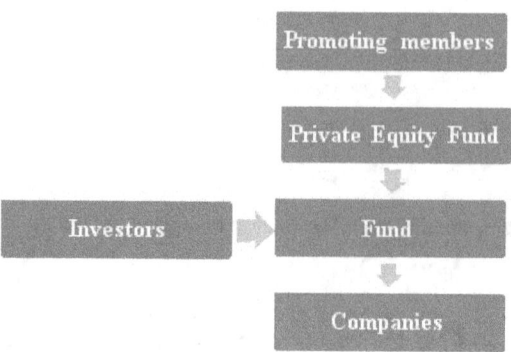

Source: my processing

Private equity investments are usually categorized considering the life cycle phase of the target company:

- *Start-up* investments[5] in companies, in the early stage of their life, that need backing to fund the development of the new business idea or concept (also called venture capital investments);
- *Expansion* investments[6] in companies, with a brief history behind them and good growth prospects, in need of capital to fund their developing businesses, aimed to expand the production activity;
- *Replacement* investments[7] in the later stages of developed businesses, aimed at restructuring the shareholder base. The private equity fund substitutes one or more minority shareholders no longer interested in pursuing the activity;
- *Buy-out* investments are the largest category of private equity investments and consist in the acquisition of a company's ownership, or a minority stake. A buy-out often takes place by using a large amount of borrowed money[8].

The goal of any private equity fund is to achieve, in the medium-long term, capital gain through the enhancement and then sale of the portfolio company. However, the world financial crisis that started in 2008 and the consequent credit tightening hit the private equity market causing a banking credit crunch that does not allow any more high-leveraged transactions.

These changes in the financial market are prompting investors to use the operational improvement as a tool of value creation instead of financial-leverage. The presence of a professional investor in the capital of a company can accelerate the growth plans of the company by providing managerial and organizational skills through the introduction of planning and control systems of business results that increase the communication quality of the portfolio company.

"Although the ability to raise debt will remain an important component of private equity investing, the sharp decline of financial-leverage in the global financial system has reduced private equity funds' ability to create value through financial engineering. As a result, private equity funds have become even more dependent on their ability to improve operational performance in every transaction to achieve their investment goals and generate attractive returns."[9]

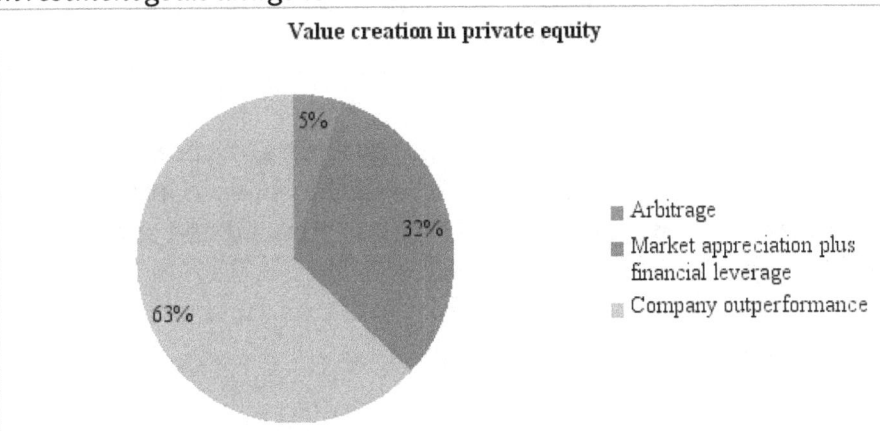

Value creation in private equity

- Arbitrage
- Market appreciation plus financial leverage
- Company outperformance

5%

32%

63%

Source: The McKinsey Quarterly, 2005 Number 1. "Why some PE firms do better than others."

A 2005 McKinsey & Co. study of private equity firms revealed that "company outperformance" was the main driver of value creation in almost two-thirds of the transaction, while "market appreciation plus financial leverage" was identified as about one third and "arbitrage" driving value creation in about 5%[10].

Funds usually last between 8 and 10 years. This period may be decomposed into two different times: the investment period and the divestment period, until the end of the fund, in which the subsidiaries are sold.

The divestment phase is the final part of the investment process. The main divestment strategies are:

- *IPO*: the sale of the assets to public investors via an initial public offering. It can result in a substantial increase in valuation through the initial boost provided by financial leverage so that the magnification of final returns can be very significant. In my opinion, this should be the preferred route to realize value in particular for private equity funds that undertake buyout investments;
- *Trade sale*: the sale of the assets to a strategic buyer that operates in the same industry;
- *Secondary buy out*: the sale of the assets to another private equity fund;
- *Buy back*: the reacquisition of the assets by the original shareholder.

Private equity fund usually sells the shares of a portfolio company once the value-creation process has been completed. Of course, not all investments work out as planned and some assets will be disposed as *written off*.

% Distribution by type of divestments in the first half of 2012 (Italy)

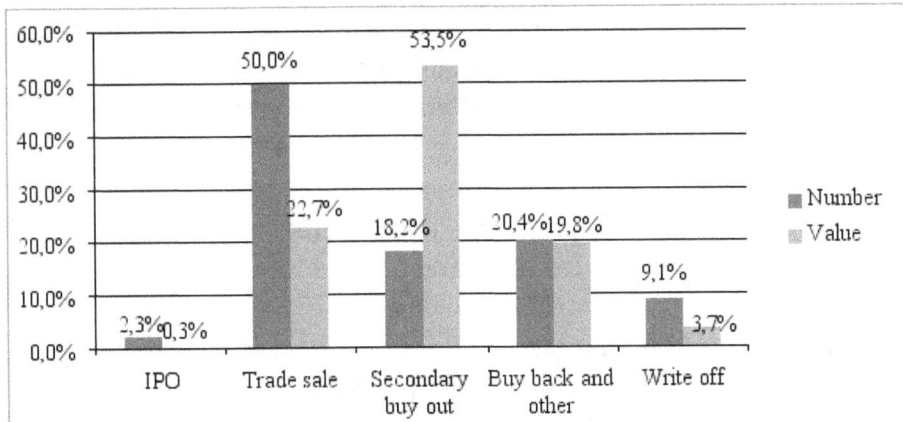

Source: Survey AIFI – PricewaterhouseCoopers (Adapted)

According the chart, most of the divestments that took place in Italy in the first semester of 2012, were performed by selling assets to strategic buyers, with a value of 22.7%, compared to the value of the other kind of exits performed in the period. Secondary buy-outs had the highest divestment value although they were not many in terms of number.

1.2 A short summary of private equity in USA and comparison with Italy

The history of private equity in USA is characterized by a series of cycles of expansion and contraction from the mid-20th century. Since the origins of modern private equity industry in 1946, there have been four major periods:

- *Early history*[11]: it was characterized by relatively small volumes of investments in private equity because of limited awareness and familiarity with the private equity industry. The first two venture capital firms in 1946 were ARDC[12] and J.H. Whitney & Company. During the 1960s and 1970s, venture capital firms focused their investment activity primarily on starting and expanding electronic companies. As a result, venture capital came to be synonymous with technology finance.

- *The 1980s*: it was characterized by a considerable increase in leveraged buyout activity financed by junk bonds. The beginning of the first boom period in private equity was marked by the success of the Gibson Greetings acquisition in 1982 by Wesray Capital Corporation and ending with the massive buyout of RJR Nabisco in 1989 by KKR[13], before the near collapse of the leveraged buyout industry in the late 1980s and early 1990s. In 1980, the private equity industry raised approximately $2.4 billion of annual investor commitments and by the end of the decade, in 1989, this figure stood at $21.9 billion.

- *The 1990s*: it began after the savings and loan crisis, the insider trading scandals, the real estate market collapse and recession of the early 1990s. This period saw the appearance of more institutionalized private equity firms, ultimately culminating in the huge dot-com bubble in 1999 and 2000. Among the highest profile technology companies with venture capital backing were Amazon.com, America Online, E-bay, Intuit, Macromedia, Netscape, Sun Microsystems and Yahoo! In 1992, the private equity industry raised approximately $20.8 billion of annual investor commitments and in 2000 reached $305.7 billion.

- *The 2000s*: it began after the collapse of the dot-com bubble. The NASDAQ crash that started in March 2000 shook the entire venture capital industry and valuations for start-up technology companies. In 2003, the private equity industry had spent the previous two and a half years to recover from losses in telecommunications and technology companies. In 2004 and 2005, major buyouts once again become common such as Dollarama, Toys "R" Us, the Hertz Corporation, Metro-Goldwyn-Mayer and SunGard. In 2007, leveraged buyouts reached unprecedented sizes as the Blackstone Group's initial public offering. In 2008 began the worst financial crisis since the Great Depression of the 1930s. In late 2009, the consensus among industry members was that private equity firms will need to become more like asset managers, offering buyouts as just part of their portfolio, in order to prosper. The industry must also become better in adding value by operational improvements rather than pure financial engineering.

Private equity investing has increasingly spread across the

world. The follow figure shows the distribution of private equity investments across the world in 2005.

Private equity investments throughout the world: 2005

1%	22%	1%	40%	35%

Source: PriceWaterhouseCoopers Global Private Equity Report 2006

Top 20 Countries (based on investment) US$ Billion (2005)

Country Ranking	Investment Value	Funds Raised
1. USA	46.41	159.00
2. UK	27.92	53.48
3. China	8.81	2.14
4. France	8.55	13.42
5. Japan	7.95	4.42
6. Singapore	4.41	0.74
7. Sweden	3.52	2.25
8. Germany	3.16	3.37
9. Spain	3.12	1.20
10. Netherlands	2.74	2.86
11. Italy	2.56	1.58
12. Australia	2.32	2.08
13. Korea	2.10	2.52

14. India	1.94	2.48
15. Denmark	1.24	1.17
16. Canada	1.24	1.49
17. Israel	1.08	1.34
18. South Africa	0.89	0.40
19. New Zealand	0.75	0.22
20. Indonesia	0.56	-

Source: PriceWaterhouseCoopers Global Private Equity Report 2006

In Italy, private equity investing can be traced back to May 1986, when the Italian Private Equity and Venture Capital Association (AIFI)[14] has been created. With the passing of time, the number and range of operators has evolved in relation to changes in the economic and financial environment and the legal framework.

Until 1986, banks were not allowed to acquire shares of companies. It was only with the CICR[15] decision of 6 February 1987 that banks were allowed to invest in private equity but only through _merchant banking_ companies; however, they could not take control of the investee companies. A fundamental step for the development of the private equity industry was the CICR decision of 11 June 1993 that establishes closed-end funds. Over time, closed-end funds become the main instrument to carry out investment activities in the risk capital of unlisted companies[16].

The expansion of private equity has been fast since the nineties and a growth process is still ongoing. Between 1986 and 1996, a limited number of operators invested in the private equity industry, but a real development of this sector can be observed between 1997 and 2001 when the diffusion of new ICT[17] has attracted financial resources. Then followed a period of relative stability until 2005, when a new cycle of further development of the sector began.

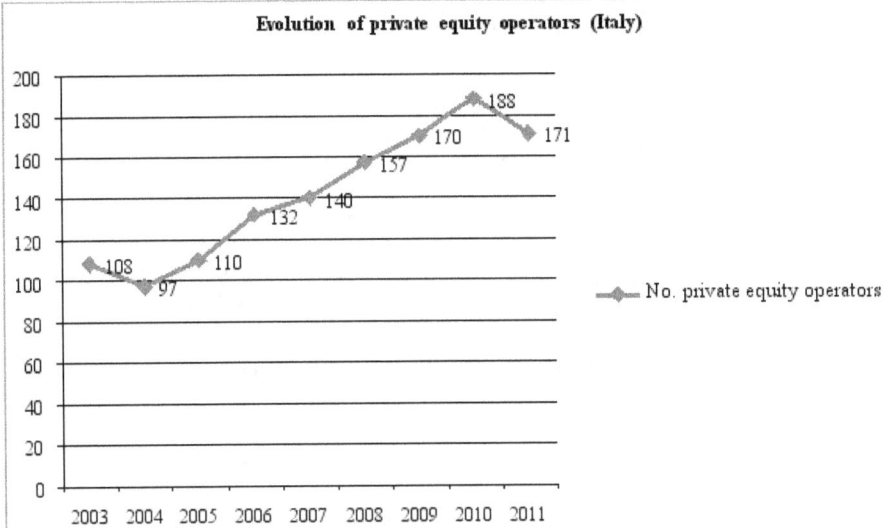

Source: AIFI – PricewaterhouseCoopers (Adapted)

The main categories of private equity operators are:

- Italian closed-end funds managed by SGR[18]: A closed-end investment fund is an investment company that raises a fixed amount of capital by issuing a fixed number of shares that are purchased by investors. The Bank of Italy authorizes the holding company to carry out investment activities by a closed-end private equity fund. Private equity holding companies are listed in the register of financial intermediaries held by the Bank of Italy[19];
- Funds specialized in the early stage;
- Pan European funds;
- Italian banks and their subsidiaries;
- Public and regional investors;
- Investment companies.

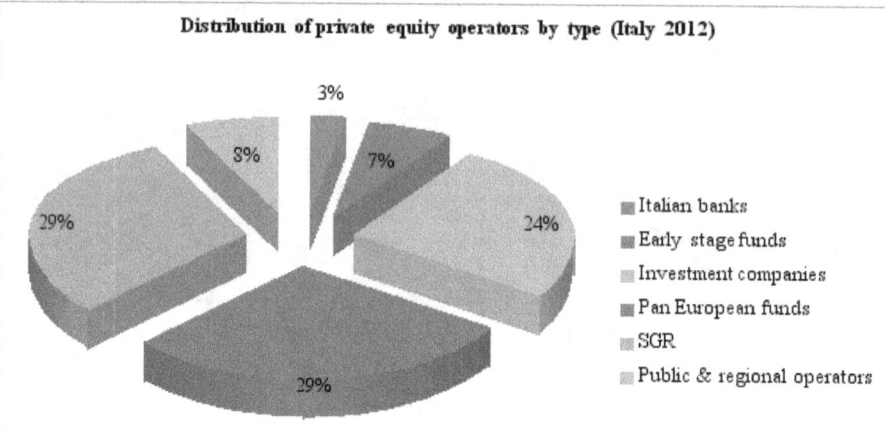

Distribution of private equity operators by type (Italy 2012)

- Italian banks
- Early stage funds
- Investment companies
- Pan European funds
- SGR
- Public & regional operators

Source: Survey AIFI – PricewaterhouseCoopers (Adapted)

The range of private equity operators has changed with the passing of time: at the beginning, the activity was mostly promoted by local operators. At present, thanks to the expansion of the market, the universe of players is made up of Italian and international banks, Italian closed-end funds (SGR), Pan European funds, Public operators and other minor investors.

In the mid-nineties SGR closed-end funds, established by the Law n. 344 of 14 August 1993, has begun to operate. These companies were only 1% of private equity operators at the end of 1994 and then reached about 30% at the end of 2007.

Even banks have seen a remarkable expansion in the late eighties, up to count, in terms of private equity operators, for about 50% of the market and then settling on a share of about 30% in the late nineties. After 2000, the presence of banks on the total number of private equity operators began to decline due to the creation of many closed-end funds issued by the same banking groups.

Recently, this trend was interrupted by a reduction in the number of SGR promoted by banks and an increase of independent operators' importance. Even public operators, national and regional, represent a significant market share, especially in start-up and expansion operations.

In Italy, the most recent data indicate a greater spread of closed-end funds used to manage private equity investment. At the end of December 2007 were authorized 60 SGR, which controlled 98 closed-end funds.

The number of SGR authorized to manage closed funds increased progressively since the entry into force of the TUF[20], which has expanded operational flexibility in the management of these funds. Compared to all private equity operators, SGR accounted for just fewer than 8% in 1995, to 15% in 1998 and almost 30% at the end of December 2007.

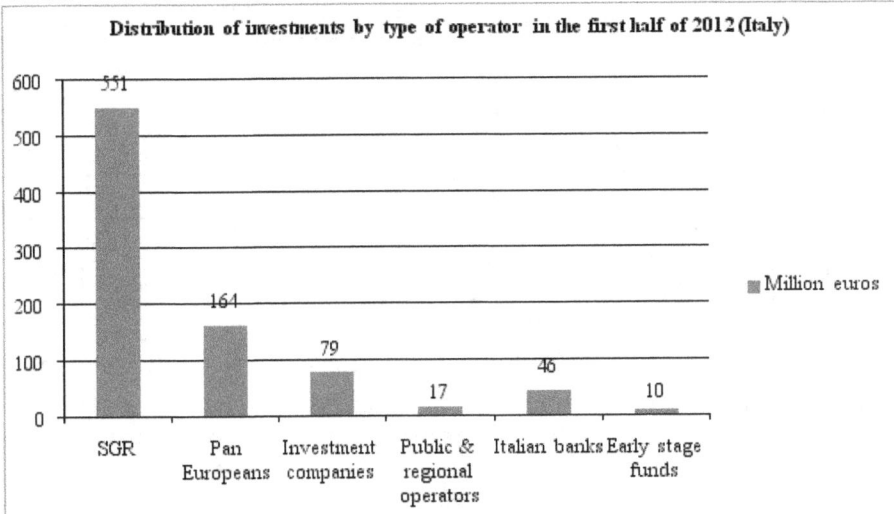

Source: Survey AIFI – PricewaterhouseCoopers (Adapted)

1.3 Private equity performance

According to an analysis on the performance of Italian private equity funds carried out by KPMG[21], a common way used to evaluate private equity funds' performance is the Internal Rate of Return (IRR[22]). This analysis has been carried out considering Gross Pooled IRR on Realized Investments, which provides a "realistic" overview of the market and represents the overall performance related to the divestments carried out, but it does not take into account the implied yield referred to the investments still held in portfolio. Performances have been measured in terms of Pooled IRR, given all the cash flow reported by private equity funds, aggregated as if they were the result of operations carried out by a "single fund".

In Italy, since 1986, that is considered the year in which private equity activity has begun, more than 1,000 divestments have been performed. As shown in the table below, the historical performance showed a 26.3% Pooled IRR and an average investment of Euro 8.7 million in the period 1986-2011.

Historical IRR since inception analysis (Italy)

	1986-2011
N. of PE & VC houses presenting realized investments	101
N. of realized investments since inception	1,087
Average investment size (Euro mln)	8.7
Total Cash Out (Euro mln)	9,491
Total Cash In (Euro mln)	16,597
Yearly Pooled IRR	**26.3%**

Source: KPMG Corporate Finance

Historical IRR since inception analysis: annual Cash In / Cash Out related to realized investments (Italy)

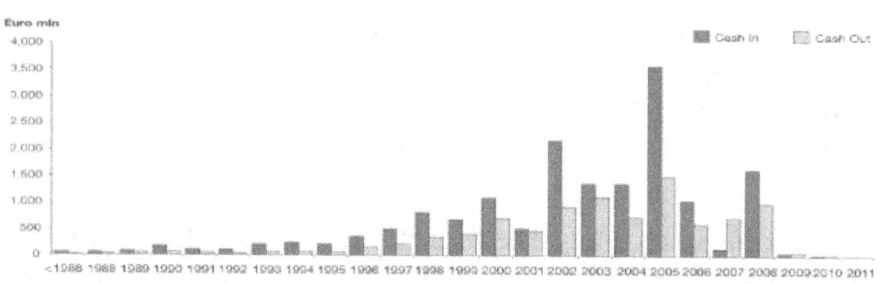

Source: KPMG Corporate Finance

The historical analyses show that MBO/MBI operations are the top performer, with an average IRR of over 43%. As shown in the tables below, most of all transactions involved minority stakes, while the holding period of the majority of realized investments is around 4 years.

Historical IRR since inception distribution by financing

stage (Italy)

	1986-2011			
	Early Stage	Development	MBO/MBI	Replacement
N. of transactions	99	407	318	125
Yearly Pooled IRR	28.2%	15.7%	43.4%	27.3%

Source: KPMG Corporate Finance

Historical IRR since inception distribution by acquired stakes (Italy)

	1986-2011				
	< 5%	5%-10%	10%-25%	25%-50%	> 50%
N. of transactions	108	127	296	285	133
Incidence	11%	13%	31%	30%	14%
Yearly Pooled IRR	14.9%	23.0%	17.0%	29.2%	38.9%

Source: KPMG Corporate Finance

Historical IRR since inception distribution by time gap between first investment and divestment (Italy)

	1986-2011					
	< 2	2-3	3-4	4-5	5-7	> 7
N. of transactions	237	237	167	133	199	114
Incidence	22%	22%	15%	12%	18%	10%
Yearly Pooled IRR	82.0%	53.4%	51.4%	18.2%	6.7%	6.6%

Source: KPMG Corporate Finance

Private equity have had a positive impact on the Italian economy during the period between 1999 and 2006, in fact backed companies have higher performances as compared to the main economic indicators. As shown in the two charts below, revenue's growth of private equity backed companies was significantly higher than GDP[23] growth and employment's growth rate in private equity backed companies was higher than the Italian employment growth rate as well.

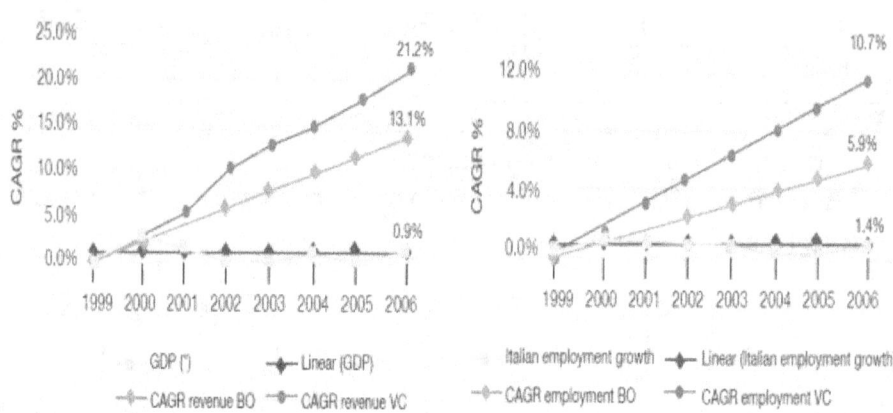

Source: ISTAT and PricewaterhouseCoopers analysis

The primary reason to invest in private equity is the expectation of a higher return than other securities available on the traditional market. In my opinion, the higher return should be justified by the less liquidity than other types of equity investments in listed companies. As the chart shows, in the medium term the private equity funds have historically shown significantly higher returns than those of publicly traded stocks.

Private Equity Performance Compared to S&P 500 (as of Sept. 30, 2011)

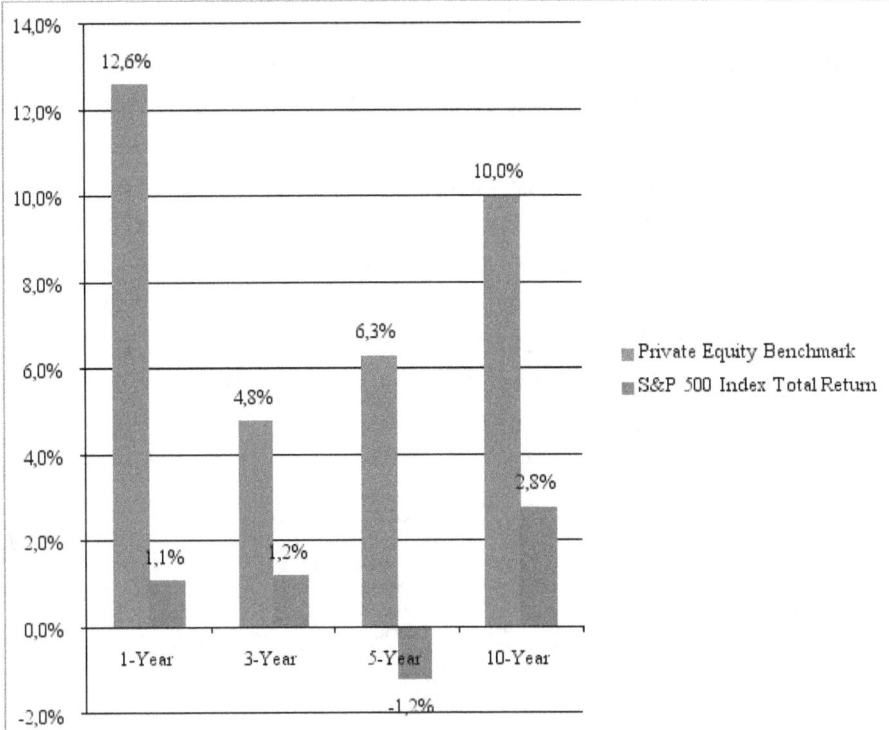

Source: Private Equity Growth Capital Council, *Private Equity Performance Updated,* April 3, 2012 (Adapted)

On the 3rd of April 2012, the Private Equity Growth Capital Council (PEGCC)[24] released a new analysis highlighting superior returns provided by private equity investing compared to the S&P 500[25]. The research shows private equity outperformed the S&P 500 for 1, 3, 5, and 10-year time horizons respectively by 11.5, 3.6, 7.5 and 7.2 percentage points[26]. These are substantial premiums and are clearly a prime reason for the increasing interest from institutional investors.

1.4 Expansion in Italy

Expansion is the phase of the business cycle when a company wants to develop further the production and sales; in this stage, the company usually defines a growth project with a specific roadmap and estimates the financial requirements of the project.

Small and medium-sized enterprises are a crucial component

of the Italian economy. This segment includes in fact the vast majority of existing companies on the territory that, in my opinion, are too small to be competitive and face international rivals. From the second half of 2008, Italy has been hit by the economic and financial crisis that has rapidly affected the entire globe. I think that other factors contribute to this lack of growth, which in turn would develop into a vicious cycle, involving politics, bureaucracy, and lack of trust in institutions. In my opinion, these factors would cause a loss of growth potential from the failure to capitalize on the competencies of Italian industries.

Italy country competitiveness

The most problematic factors for doing business

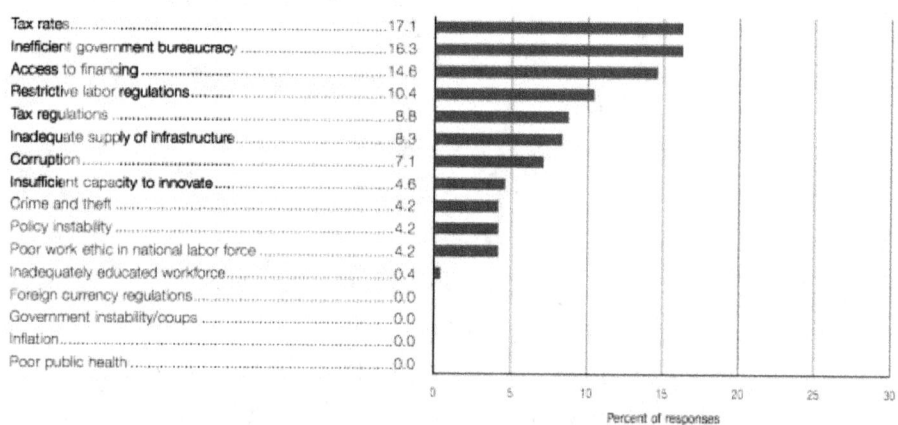

Tax rates	17.1
Inefficient government bureaucracy	16.3
Access to financing	14.6
Restrictive labor regulations	10.4
Tax regulations	8.8
Inadequate supply of infrastructure	8.3
Corruption	7.1
Insufficient capacity to innovate	4.6
Crime and theft	4.2
Policy instability	4.2
Poor work ethic in national labor force	4.2
Inadequately educated workforce	0.4
Foreign currency regulations	0.0
Government instability/coups	0.0
Inflation	0.0
Poor public health	0.0

Percent of responses

Note: From the list of factors above, respondents were asked to select the five most problematic for doing business in their country and to rank them between 1 (most problematic) and 5. The bars in the figure show the responses weighted according to their rankings.

Source: Alberti Fernando G.: "The Italian way of doing industry", February 27, 2013

As shown in the graph above, one of the most problematic factors in doing business is the "access to financing" with a percentage of 14,6%.

It is statistically proven that in Italy the crisis has had a profoundly negative impact on small and medium enterprises, which have seen a sharp decline in sales, in the production, employment, and exports.

The greatest problems remain in relation to the financial structure, which reflects a liquidity sharply deteriorated, reducing turnover, elongation of the payment's time and a compli-cated access to credit.

Italy is largely made up of small and medium-sized fam-ily businesses, many of which have traditionally preferred bank credit to grow their business because of reluctance to admit out-side influences. According to Danilo Masoni and Simon Meads[27], the debt crisis in Europe has revealed that Italian banks are among the weakest in Europe and banks such as UniCredit had to revise loan agreements, cutting credit lines to those who seek to increase their capital levels. In addition, new rules to guarantee the stability of the banking system, known as Basel III[28], have im-posed many restrictions that, in my opinion, could increase the risk of a credit crunch, especially if implemented in a period of economic recession.

Consequently, always according to Danilo Masoni and Simon Meads, the Italian companies that are based on short-term debt more than elsewhere in Europe are forced to rethink their busi-ness models as an important cultural change. The slow economy and tight bank credit would reduce the traditional reluctance of family businesses to consider institutional investors as less a threat and more as the value for the skills they can bring to com-panies that are struggling to grow in times of economic crisis.

In this context, I think that Italian companies have many limi-tations to expand their activities for the impossibility of obtain-ing finance. In my opinion, additional equity capital allows com-panies to expand their products and markets. Companies that need more equity capital than can be provided by their owners could approach private equity investors.

A company wanting to raise equity capital has to get private equity investors interested in investing in it. The main factor is the type of business that the company is in and how attractive is to private equity investors.

Therefore, the attention of private equity funds has moved on small and medium-sized enterprises. This is demonstrated by the fact that, as shown in the two graphs below, "expansion" is the most common type of operation and, in recent years, it became the most target investment of the fund raising activity.

Evolution of the fund raising distribution by type of target investment (Italy)

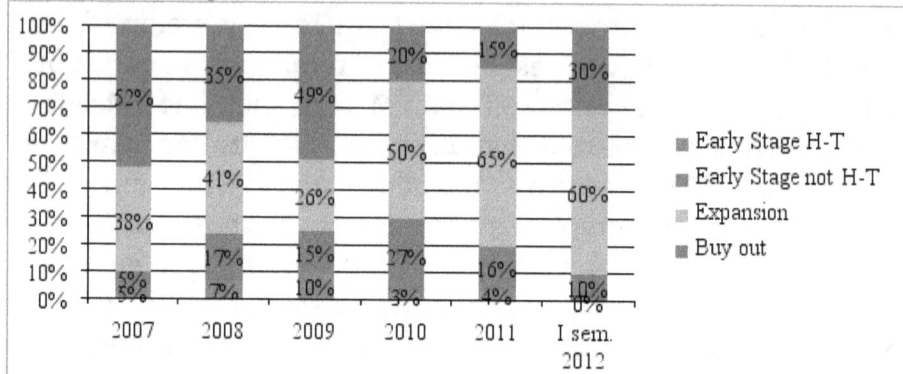

Source: Survey AIFI – PricewaterhouseCoopers (Adapted)

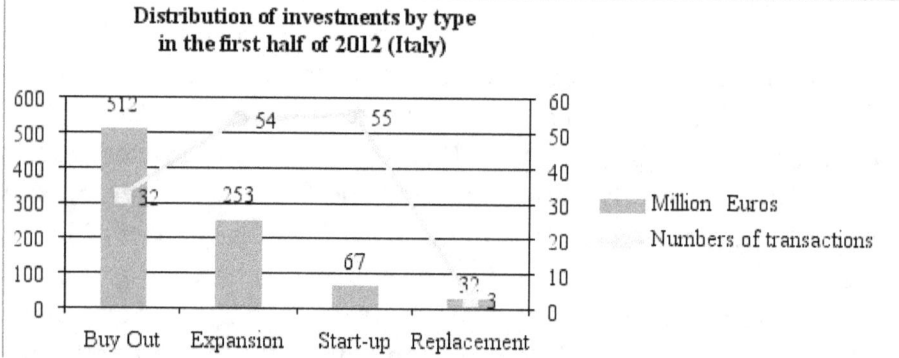

Source: Survey AIFI – PricewaterhouseCoopers (Adapted)

The graph reports the distribution of investments in Italy during the first semester 2012. The majority of the transactions were represented by small and medium size investments in start-up companies (about 1.2 million euros/transaction) and expansion capital deals (about 4.7 million euros/transaction). Buy-outs (about 16 million euros/transaction) and replacements (about 11 million euros/transaction) counted only for 31% in terms of number of operations, but buy-outs had definitely the highest investment size among all categories.

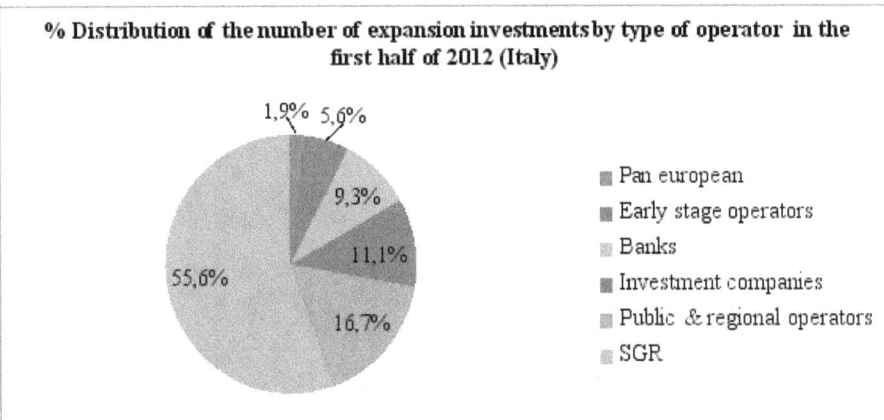

% Distribution of the number of expansion investments by type of operator in the first half of 2012 (Italy)

Source: Survey AIFI – PricewaterhouseCoopers (Adapted)

The pie chart shows the percentage distribution of the number of expansion operations in Italy by type of operator during the first semester 2012. From the pie chart, it is possible to see that more than half of expanding operations are run by SGR (55.6%), while banks have carried out only 9.3% of expansion operations.

In fact, on 18 March 2010, on the initiative of the Italian Ministry of Economy and Finance and representatives of the major Italian banking groups, was set up the FII[29] with initial funding of € 1 billion to be allocated to support small and medium-sized enterprises. The FII was created with the aim to facilitate small and medium-sized Italian companies to increase their market share, especially in the international arena.

In the first year of operation, the FII has realized 18 direct investments in companies of approximately 10.4 million euro for each and 9 indirect investments in private equity funds of approximately 21 million euro for each. Within direct investments, 6 companies operate in machine tools and equipment, 4 in services, 3 in consumer goods, 2 in shipping and shipbuilding, 1 in biomedical and pharmaceutical, 1 in industrial components and 1 in ICT. Among the 9 investment funds, 5 have a geographical distribution that includes the entire Italian territory, while the remaining 4 have only a regional geographical distribution[30].

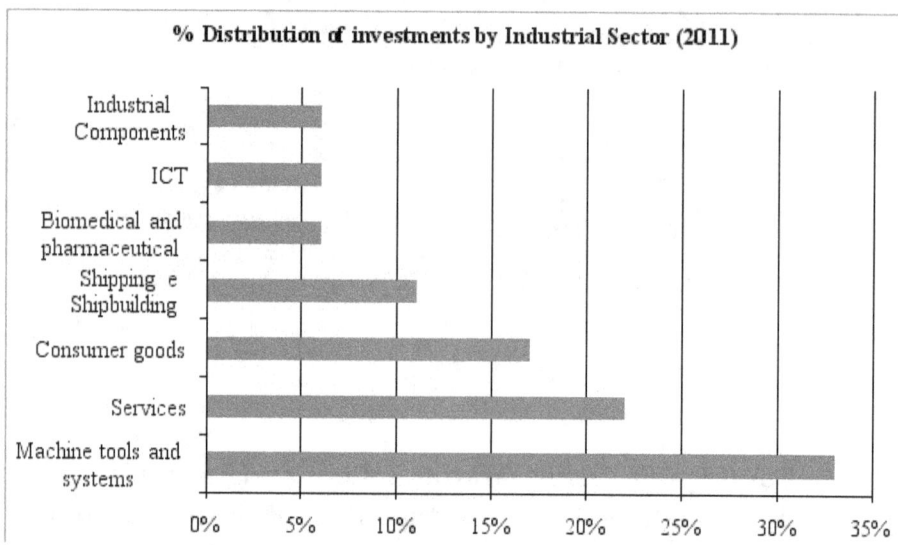

% Distribution of investments by Industrial Sector (2011)

Source: Fondo Italiano d'Investimento, Annual Report as of December 31, 2011

In the next chapter, I will examine a case study concerning an expansion operation implemented by Antares Private Equity on a small company that operates in the home entertainment industry: Chili SPA.

I will start with a brief company overview and then I will go on to analyze the home entertainment industry in which it operates. After that, I will analyze the company externally and internally, through the Porter's five forces analysis and SWOT analysis, evaluating the current strategy and then the results obtained in the first year of operation. Finally, I will make assumptions about future strategies.

CHAPTER 2. THE CASE OF CHILI S.P.A.

2.1 A real case of expansion

The present chapter deals with an expansion capital operation performed by an Italian private equity operator. The target company is Chili S.p.A., a company that stems from a management buy-out from Fastweb, the largest alternative fixed-line telecommunications provider in Italy. In 2010, the same managers who have developed the first IPTV platform worldwide have started developing a technological platform for the distribution of video on demand. In June 2012, Fastweb spun-off its VoD business unit founding a new company: Chili S.p.A.. The company's offer consists of a wide range of movies available for purchase or rental, together with some free contents, available on its website[31]. There is not any entry fee but on Chili, customers pay only what they want to see. Becoming independent from Fastweb, Chili can move freely on the market and take advantage of every growth opportunity.

The shareholders of the newly created Chili S.p.A. are the managers that had developed the idea inside Fastweb: Stefano Parisi (President), Giorgio Tacchia (CEO), Alessandro Schintu (Head of Marketing & Communication) and Stefano Flamia (Technical Manager).

In July 2012, few months after the buy-out, Antares Private Equity, thorough an expansion capital deal, acquired the 15.4% of Chili providing cash to boost the company's growth.

The following chart represents the actual company's ownership structure:

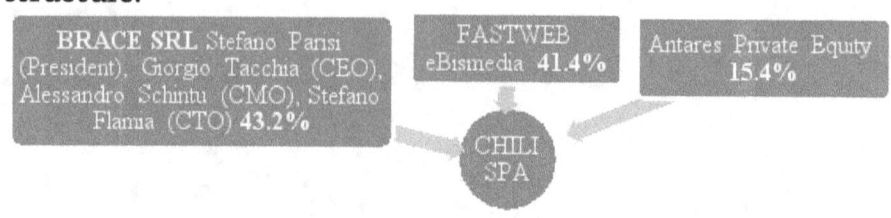

Source: Antares Private Equity

The reasons that led Antares to invest in Chili are:

-   The belief in the project, in its management, the potential growth of distribution of Smart TVs and other devices like tablet and smartphones. Moreover, in Italy the home entertainment market is characterized by a significant lack of players, mainly because of Blockbuster's bankruptcy. Chili can also be seen as an alternative to piracy, providing better quality at a reasonable price. Chili is in a position to expand right now most of its potential. The goal is that Chili becomes the reference point for film lovers. Customers are able to download movies anytime: full on demand proposition available at any single time;
-   everywhere: plug and play solution for any digital platform, multiscreen, available at home and in mobility;
-   everything: huge catalogue and many contents for free, there is always something for everyone;
-   any connectivity: no boundaries, any broadband line up to 1Mb, any connected device off-the-shelf;
-   High quality: Full-HD, ready for 3D, handled by the best in class on network expertise.

To ensure Chili's profitability is essential to assess strategically the complex panorama of the home entertainment industry, and then use this information to gain a competitive advantage over competitors. However, the definition of home entertainment industry presents challenges because movies and television programs are distributed to viewers across a wide spectrum of channels: DVD rental in retail stores or online, TV with premium channels, pay-per-view, video on demand (VOD), and Internet.

2.2 Home Entertainment industry

Nowadays, despite the economic crisis, the technological equipment used by families has improved. However, there is a wide cultural and geographical gap that makes our country still far from the standards of the major European countries. Families made up of people older than 65 years old continue to be away from new technologies, while families with at least one minor are, on the contrary, more "technological".

The mobile phone is now present in the 92.4% of families and the most common new technological devices among Italian families are the DVD player (59.4%) and the personal computer (59.3%). Internet access is available in 55.5% of families and 48.6% of them have a broadband connection. Less common are the satellite dish (33.8%), smartphones (34.7%), cameras (25.2%) and game consoles (20.3%).

Since 2011, the percentage of families with a broadband connection has increased from 45.8% to 48.6%. In addition, the number of families with a smartphone has registered a growth: from 33.1% to 34.7%. On the contrary, the number of families who own a satellite dish has decreased (from 36.4% to 33.8%), as well as the once owning a DVD player (from 63.2% to 59.4%) and a camera (from 28.3% to 25, 2%).

Italians' technological goods (%)

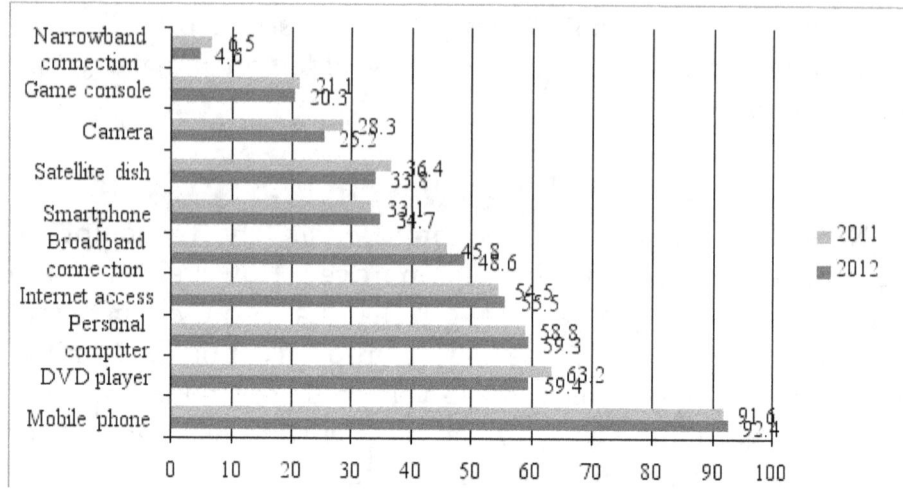

Source: ISTAT

According to NPD DisplaySearch[32], in 2012 237 million Smart TVs were sold worldwide, observing a decrease of 4 percent compared to 2011. The research estimates that in 2013 sales will not increase significantly. NPD DisplaySearch published an estimate of the number of provisions related to Smart TV's market from now until 2016: in 2013, sales are expected to be more or less the same as in 2012 while from 2014 onwards a new growth is expected, although still at lower rates than those recorded until 2011.

TVs' sales

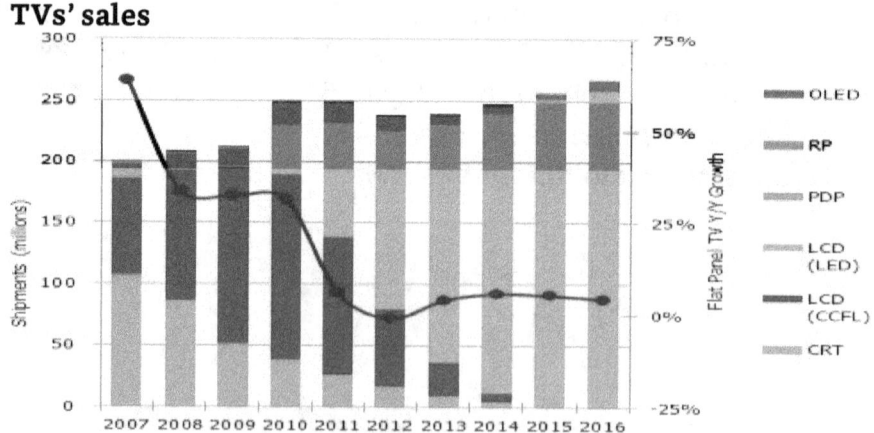

Source: NPD DisplaySearch

An Altroconsumo's[33] survey named "why people buy a smart

TV?" indicates that in Italy just only 7% of people who bought a smart TV connected the device to the internet. The main reason why most people buy these new smart TVs is simply to replace old TVs, considering the fact that both producers and sellers direct customers to buy smart TVs.

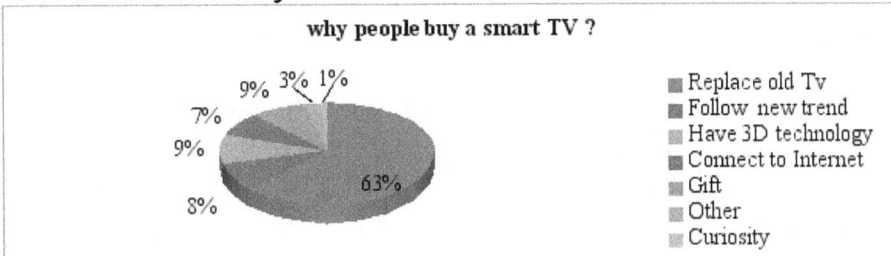

why people buy a smart TV ?

- Replace old Tv
- Follow new trend
- Have 3D technology
- Connect to Internet
- Gift
- Other
- Curiosity

Source: Altroconsumo

Italians' expense in the home entertainment amounts to 486 million euro in 2011 and is steadily falling since 2007. In 2011, sales represented 58% of home entertainment's total turnover while newsstands were 27% and rentals were only 15%. Blu-ray Disc is gaining importance by representing approximately 17% of sales (excluding newsstand) at the end of 2011[34].

Italians' expense in movies					
in millions euros					
	2007	2008	2009	2010	2011
Sales	443	382	334	336	281
DVD	436	368	321	295	232
Blue ray disc	3	11	23	40	49
Others	4	2	0,7	0,6	0,2
News-stand	307	261	201	164	130
Total sales + news-stand	750	642	545	500	411
Rental	218	161	115	90	75
Total expense	**968**	**803**	**660**	**590**	**486**
Of which online (in % on total)	n.d.	n.d.	n.d.	0,4%	1,8%
Piracy	n.d.	n.d.	n.d.	380	380
Total potential market	**n.d.**	**n.d.**	**n.d.**	**970**	**866**

Source: Milano Finanza: "Scommessa dei fondi sui film online", 13th July

In 2011, results confirmed the ability of the home entertainment industry to exploit new opportunities offered by technological innovation, such as the success of the Blu-ray Disc and the appearance of on-line Video on Demand. Nowadays online Video on Demand has a marginal weight in home entertainment's total sales, due to the less experience of the Italian population with new technologies, particularly among older people, and the delay of our country in terms of infrastructure. However, on-line Video on Demand is an opportunity for the home entertainment industry to increase the total turnover by exploiting legal systems that will replace piracy.

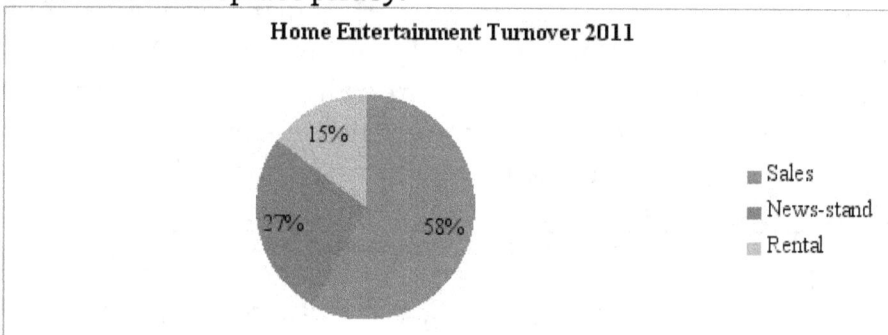

Home Entertainment Turnover 2011

Source: my processing

Italians' expense in movies (in million euros)

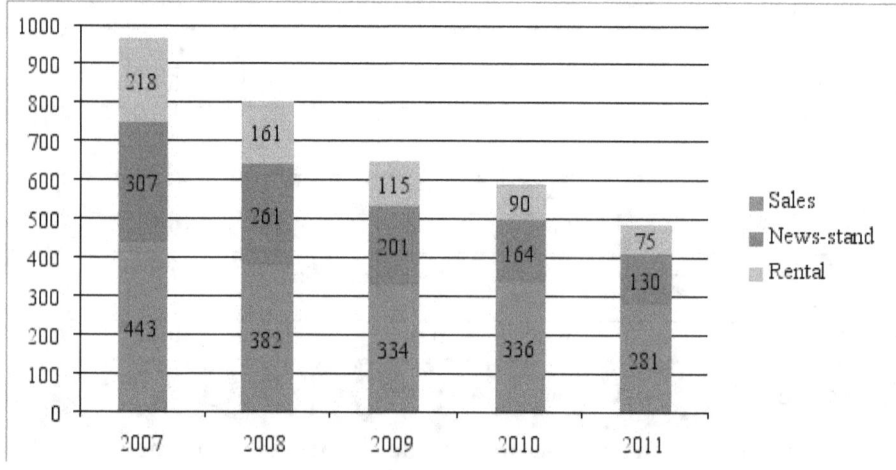

Source: my processing

DVD's rentals are suffering a lot compared to other forms of entertainment, such as piracy, used in particular by young people. Also because of piracy, a progressively smaller percentage of people rent DVDs. The considerable increase of piracy contents over the last years has strongly reduced the customer spending; this has inevitably reduced stores profitability with the consequent closing of several stores and led players such as Blockbuster that was the global leader of the physical support distribution to bankruptcy. Chili is trying to exploit the space freed up from blockbuster chains and to capture part of the piracy market, pushing on quality of contents and multi-screen experience.

There are three types of piracy: physical piracy, digital piracy, indirect piracy. The physical piracy consists in buying counterfeit DVDs on the street or from a friend. Digital piracy occurs when you download not original movies directly from the Internet, when you watch movies in streaming, when you download fake movies using peer-to-peer software or when you swap digital copies. Indirect piracy occurs when you receive a fake DVD as gift or when you watch fake movies at a friends' house[35].

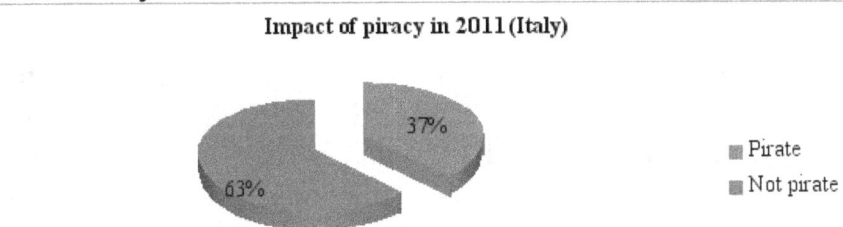

Impact of piracy in 2011 (Italy)

37%

63%

- Pirate
- Not pirate

Source: FAPAV, Pirateria: scenario 2011

There are many reasons why people buy counterfeit movies:

1. *Saving*: people prefer to spend less money on a movie rather than going to the cinema, buy a DVD or rent it.
2. *Practicality*: people want to be able to obtain movies without leaving their home and watch them whenever they want.
3. *Novelty*: people want to watch first-run movies and have

a wide range of choices.

What could offer all this legally? Online Video on Demand can.

2.3 Porter's five forces analysis

This paragraph analyzes the online Video on Demand market using Porter's Five Forces[36] as an analytical tool. Since Chili now operates only in Italy, the analyses considers the VOD industry in a local context.

<u>Entry</u>: Moderate

The online Video on Demand industry requires significant initial investments to get licenses to show movies. This kind of sunk cost can be considered as a barrier for other companies to enter the market. The technology to offer high quality contents is also a barrier to entry and requires huge investments, even if such technology is available for licensing from third parties. In this market, product differentiation takes the form of varying quality in the downloaded movies, but it should be noted that all companies should at least offer quality that is very close to DVD quality in order to ensure that the most demanding customers continue to use their service.

<u>Rivalry</u>: Low

Looking at the Italian video on demand industry, Chili faces minimal national rivalry because the industry is very concentrated and so the few market leaders that share the market, namely Acetrax and Cubovision, may engage in price competition. Although Chili faces little national rivalry in its immediate industry, the company faces an intensely competitive broader market. Since home entertainment covers a broad spectrum of technologies and channels of distribution, Chili is in direct competition with firms in a number of other industries including cable networks like Mediaset Premium and satellite companies' VOD services like SKY.

<u>Supplier Power</u>: High

Chili and its competitors buy movies from content providers that create films (such as Disney, Warner, and Paramount). The major studios have a high supplier power in the VoD market because they are the exclusive source of movies that customers desire. These highly popular movies have practically no substitutes in the rental market.

Buyer Power: Low

The bargaining power of buyers is very low in this market, because the decision of a customer to buy the service or not does not affect the overall market. Similarly, the dissatisfaction of a customer will not affect a significant amount of other customers. Overall, individual clients do not have the power to bargain for the price of the products in this market, however, prices are regulated by substitutes and preferences of customers as a whole.

Substitutes: High

The main substitutes to streaming movies are brick-and-mortar rental stores, online rentals, pay per view TV and theatres. Many people simultaneously subscribe a combination of these services, and since they are close substitutes and there are minimal switching costs, small fluctuations in prices could cause consumers to abandon one viewing format and quickly replace it with another.

2.4 SWOT analysis

The SWOT analysis is a tool of the strategic management and a great device to analyze the current strategy of an enterprise. Therefore, it is necessary to compare the company's strengths and weaknesses with the threats and opportunities. The strengths and weaknesses represent the internal environment, or more specifically, the situation inside the company. The opportunities and threats are part of the external environment, the situation outside the company. With the help of the SWOT analysis, it is possible to find out, if it is economically reasonable to pursue the ongoing strategy or to switch to another strategy.

Strengths

Entry timing: Chili entered the online video on demand market at a time when, in Italy, there were few other competitors.

Leveraging its technological leadership and its content library, that is now the widest in the country, Chili aims to be the Italian leader in the VOD distribution of content on the web.

Network connections with many partners: From the very beginning of its entry into the market, Chili has understood the importance of making partnerships with content providers and original equipment manufacturer. In fact, Chili's platform is now compatible with most hardware, operating systems and internet browsers. Movies are available at any time on any smart device (TV, PC, smartphone, tablet, Decoder Blu-Ray & Home Theatre) in Standard, High Definition and High Definition Plus as long as you have an internet connection. Chili is available on LG, Samsung, Philips, Sharp, Panasonic smart devices and Apple, Windows 8 and Android operating systems.

Very large selection of movies: The largest U.S. and Italians content providers (like DreamWorks, Warner Bros, Paramount, BIM, Eagle, MGM, Fandango, etc.) have already signed agreements with Chili allowing it to have more than 2000 movies for rental and sale. Now Chili has the largest and most diverse collection of movies of any Italian competitor. An existing variety of movies is essential in this market because consumers will frown upon not finding a movie they want to see.

Winning website formula: Differentiation exists in the type of service offered by a company: streaming movies, permanent downloads, or limited time downloads. Because the product is not easy to differentiate, the competition focuses more on the services provided with the product than the price. Chili's choice of providing streaming content and downloadable movies allows it to differentiate its service from others in the market, thus aiding Chili in its strategic positioning. In my opinion, perhaps the greatest advantage to streaming video is that it offers an even greater "instant gratification" incentive than downloadable VOD movies, as one can get the former up and running within a couple minutes with a modest connection speed, whereas a full movie download will often take about a half hour or more.

Customer satisfaction and pricing: From the beginning, Chili has understood that customers would prefer legal alternatives than download pirated movies if there was a satisfactory offer. In fact, Chili offers the possibility to rent movies at a price that ranges between € 2.95 and € 6.96 or buy them at a price that ranges between € 9.95 and € 19.95. Customers can download movies or watch them in streaming and they can pay by credit card, electronic wallet or PayPal. Chili's competitive advantage is that customers do not need to take out a subscription, but they pay only for what they watch.

Weaknesses

Lack of global diversification: Although Chili is available everywhere in Italy, now its web site does not work outside the country. The business may take advantage from globalization, providing greater stability and raising the prospects for growth.

Opportunities

Fill the gap in the market: After Blockbuster's bankruptcy, a vacuum has been created in the Italian market and no one has not filled it yet. Chili's opportunity is precisely to fill that vacuum before someone else does, through its varied range of movies, downloadable or streaming visible from its website, and to become the undisputed leader in the Italian VOD industry.

Threats

Competitors are the clearest threats for Chili. Beyond this, customer satisfaction is the only aspect of this business that can make or break a company. In this section, I examine the main Chili Italian and foreign competitors.

- Vudu distributes full-length movies over the internet to television in the United States of America. Walmart acquired it in March 2010 from two private equity companies Greylock Partners and Benchmark Capital.
- Acetrax is an English-Swiss Video on Demand Company that was bought by Sky. The company provides over-the-top content in Europe (Italy included), for Samsung, Panasonic, LG and Toshiba's smart TVs.
- LoveFilm is a UK-based provider of home video and video game rental through DVD-by-mail and stream-

ing video on demand in the UK, Germany and Scandinavia. It is an Amazon.com subsidiary. In January 2012, LoveFilm announced that it had reached 2 million subscribers.

- Netflix is an American provider of on-demand Internet streaming media in North and South America, the Caribbean, United Kingdom, Ireland, Sweden, Denmark, Norway, Finland and flat rate DVD-by-mail in the United States. In April 2011, Netflix announced 23.6 million subscribers in the United States and over 26 million worldwide.
- Cubovision is an Italian online television and video on demand service, owned by Telecom Italia, which allow you to buy movies and TV series individually or by subscription. It has 27 channels and wide free programs.
- Hulu is an internet service offering video on demand movies and TV shows, especially NBC, FOX and other cable networks. Currently the service is offered only in the United States.

CONCLUSION

The conclusion drawn from this paper, in spite find solid foundation in the theoretical premises presented, are not intended to establish itself as absolute, but are the result of analysis aimed at identifying the benefits arising from the use of private equity. In this work, after defining what is private equity and having outlined the salient points of his history, I continued on the analysis of performances and features of expanding operations in Italy. Finally, in this work, I analyzed the case of Chili SPA, a company that operates in the online Video on Demand industry.

Even in the midst of difficult economic conditions, there could be many opportunities for private equity firms to generate value in companies they buy by implementing operational improvements through a combination of experience and expertise. One of these opportunities could be offered by the online video on demand industry that, in my opinion, among the various industries, may be one of the most promising. In fact, American private equity funds, that few years ago started to invest in the video on demand industry, have already achieved good earnings. For example, in 2007 Providence Private Equity invested $100 million into Hulu and it sold its stake for $200 million in 2012. Private equity funds Benchmark Capital and Greylock Capital, in 2005, invested in Vudu $21 million and they sold their stake to Walmart for more than $100 million in 2010. In UK, private equity investors DFJ Esprit, Balderton Capital and Index Ventures invested in Lovefilm in 2004 and they sold their stake to Amazon for £200 million in 2011. In Italy, this kind of investment has taken place for the first time in June 2012 by Antares Private Equity through the acquisition of Chili S.p.A.

Since the video entertainment market appears to be transitioning from its current formats, physical DVD and Blu-ray technology, to digitally distributed content, it seems to me important that Chili positions itself in the Italian VOD market immediately with a good market share.

It seems reasonable to me to assume that if Chili does not gain sufficient popularity in the Italian market, it will only see diminishing market shares, especially as foreign competitors begin to invade our market.

In my opinion, to become market leader in digital video distribution Chili should adopt both short and long run strategic positions. In the short-term, Chili should focus on profitability and on the expansion of its turnover. As an instance, profitability can be increased by lowering client-acquisition costs and/or by increasing the average revenue per client.

Expanding Chili's turnover could be accomplished with competitive pricing and added product value through customer service. In the long term, it seems to me that the success of the company will depend on the production of a fast, easy-to-use, and high picture quality streaming technology. If Chili develops this streaming technology, it may have the possibility to obtain a significant competitive advantage over rivals.

REFERENCES

AIFI website: http://www.aifi.it/home.asp

ALBERTI Fernando G.: *"The Italian way of doing industry"*, February 27, 2013

Altroconsumo website: http://www.altroconsumo.it/

Antares Private Equity website: http://www.antaresinvestimenti.it/it.html

Banca d'Italia website: http://www.bancaditalia.it/

Banca d'Italia (2009), *"Il private equity in Italia"*, Questioni di Economia e Finanza, No. 41, Febbraio

Bank for International Settlements – Basel III website: http://www.bis.org/bcbs/basel3_it.htm

CARLI Stefano, *"Chili, i film online senza abbonamento, così Parisi insidia noleggio e pay-tv"*, la Repubblica – Affari & Finanza, 25 giugno 2012, p. 31

Chili SPA website: https://www.chili-tv.it/

FAPAV, *"Pirateria: scenario 2011"*

FILIPPETTI Simone, *"Stefano Parisi riparte dal cinema sul web"* Il sole 24 ore, 20 giugno 2012, p. 26

Fondo Italiano d'Investimento, *"Annual Report as of December 31, 2011"*

HEEL Joachim – KEHOE Conor, *"Why some PE firms do better than others."* The McKinsey Quarterly, 2005 Number 1

KPMG Corporate Finance website: http://www.kpmgcorporatefinance.com/

MATTHEWS Gary – BYE Mark – HOWLAND James, *"Operational Improvement: The Key to Value Creation in Private Equity."* Morgan Stanley Investment Management, July 2009

MASONI Danilo – MEADS Simon, *"Dealtalk - Italy's family firms* forced into private equity arms" REUTERS, 13th February 2012: http://uk.reuters.com/article/2012/02/13/uk-private-equity-italy-idUKTRE81C12920120213

MELONI Paolo, "La vita dopo Blockbuster: i film si noleggiano in salotto", Il Giornale, 20 giugno 2012, p. 19

NPD Displaysearch website: http://www.displaysearch.com/

ODINI Alessio, "Chili, cinema a casa 24 ore su 24", Italia Oggi, 20 giugno 2012, p. 17

PEVERARO Stefania, "Fastweb scorpora Chili e il 15% va ad Antares", Milano Finanza, 20 giugno 2012, p. 15

PEVERARO Stefania, "Scommessa dei fondi sui film online", Milano Finanza, 13 luglio 2012, p. 22

PricewaterhouseCoopers website: http://www.pwc.com/

Private Equity Growth Capital Council (PEGCC) website: http://www.pegcc.org/

Private Equity Growth Capital Council, "Private Equity Performance Updated", April 3, 2012

UNIVIDEO, "Rapporto sullo stato dell'home entertainment in Italia nel 2011"

VENTURA Gabriele, "Antares con Orrick entra in Chili Il Cinema", Italia Oggi Sette, 25 giugno 2012, p. 2

---

[1] Small and medium sized enterprises

[2] Antares Private Equity website: http://www.antaresinvestimenti.it/it.html

[3] Chili SPA website: https://www.chili-tv.it/

[4] Not publicly traded on a stock exchange

[5] Seed capital

[6] Expansion capital

[7] Distressed situation

[8] Leveraged buy-out

[9] MATTHEWS Gary – BYE Mark – HOWLAND James, "Operational Improvement: The Key to Value Creation in Private Equity." Morgan Stanley Investment Management, July 2009, page 1

[10] HEEL Joachim – KEHOE Conor, "Why some PE firms do better than others." The McKinsey Quarterly, 2005 Number 1

[11] From 1946 through 1981

[12] American Research and Development Corporation

[13] Kohlberg Kravis Roberts

[14] AIFI website: http://www.aifi.it/home.asp

[15] Comitato Interministeriale per il Credito e il Risparmio

[16] Banca d'Italia (2009), "Il private equity in Italia", Questioni di Economia e Finanza, No. 41, Febbraio

[17] Information Communication Technology

[18] Società di gestione del risparmio

[19] D. Lgs. 141/2010

[20] Testo Unico della Finanza D. Lgs. 58/98

[21] KPMG Corporate Finance website: http://www.kpmgcorporatefinance.com/

[22] The Internal Rate of Return is the discount rate that makes the net present value of all cash flows from a particular project equal to zero.

$$\sum_{t=0}^{n} \frac{F_t}{(1+IRR)^t} = 0$$

[23] Gross Domestic Product

[24] Private Equity Growth Capital Council (PEGCC) website: http://www.pegcc.org/

[25] Standard & Poor's 500, is a stock market index based on the market capitalizations of 500 leading companies publicly traded in the U.S. stock market.

[26] Private Equity Growth Capital Council, "Private Equity Performance Updated", April 3, 2012

[27] MASONI Danilo – MEADS Simon, "Dealtalk - Italy's family firms forced into private equity arms" REUTERS, 13th Febraury 2012: http://uk.reuters.com/article/2012/02/13/uk-private-equity-italy-idUKTRE81C12920120213

[28] http://www.bis.org/bcbs/basel3_it.htm

[29] Fondo Italiano di Investimento

[30] Fondo Italiano d'Investimento, "Annual Report as of December 31, 2011"

[31] http://www.chili-tv.it

[32] NPD Displaysearch website: http://www.displaysearch.com/

[33] Altroconsumo website: http://www.altroconsumo.it/

[34] PEVERARO Stefania, "Scommessa dei fondi sui film online", Milano Finanza, 13 luglio 2012, p. 22

[35] FAPAV, "Pirateria: scenario 2011"

[36] Porter five forces analysis is a framework for industry analysis and business strategy development formed by Michael E. Porter of Harvard Business School in 1979.